For Patricia

The New Bride

Catherine Smith

Best wishes,
Catherine Smith.

Smith/Doorstop Books

Published 2001 by
Smith/Doorstop Books
The Poetry Business
The Studio
Byram Arcade
Westgate
Huddersfield HD1 1ND

Copyright © Catherine Smith
All Rights Reserved

ISBN 1-902382-36-6
Typeset at The Poetry Business
Printed by Swiftprint, Huddersfield

The Poetry Business gratefully acknowledges the help of
Kirklees Metropolitan Council and Yorkshire Arts.

Acknowledgements
Some of these poems were previously published in *The Daily Express, The Independent, Mslexia, The New Writer, Smiths Knoll, Soundings* and *Staple*.
In 1998 Catherine Smith received a writer's bursary from South East Arts.

Catherine Smith teaches Creative Writing for Sussex University. Her poems and short stories have been widely published and broadcast. She is working on her first novel.

This collection was a winner in The Poetry Business
Book & Pamphlet Competition 2000

CONTENTS

5	The New Bride
7	Gravid
9	Eshna's First Day
10	Marcus
11	Waiting For The Foot-Binder
12	Deck-Chairs
13	Poecilia Reticulata
14	The Real McCoy
15	Gravity
17	Picture This
18	Uncle Aubrey
19	Formica
20	Resurrection
21	Keepsakes
22	What She Sees
23	Kingfisher
24	Geography
25	Spiders
26	Stornoway Harbour
27	Sweetpeas
28	White Lies

For Jonathan, Alasdair and Liam

and also for Ros

THE NEW BRIDE

Dying, darling, is the easy bit. Fifty paracetamol,
bride-white and sticking in the throat, ten shots
of Johnny Walker, and the deed is done.
A twilight day of drowsing, then the breathing
slows to a whisper, like a sinner in Confession.

Death is dead easy. No, what happens next
is the difficulty. You bastard, howling in public,
snivelling over photos, ringing round for consolation.
And you have me burnt, like a dinner gone wrong,
you keep the charred remains of me on show

at the Wake, inviting everyone I hate. Oh God,
they come in packs, sleek as rats with platitudes
and an eye on my half of the bed, hoping to find
leftover skin, a hint of fetid breath. I leave them
no hairs on the pillow; there are none to leave.

And a year to the day since I shrug off the yoke
of life, you meet the new bride. In group therapy.
You head straight for a weeper and wailer,
telling strangers all her little tragedies. You love
the way she languishes, her tears sliming your neck,

you give into her on vile pink Austrian blinds.
The Wedding is a riot of white nylon. Everybody
drinks your health and hers, the simpering bitch.

She and Delia Smith keep you fat and happy
as a pig in shit. I want her cells to go beserk.

Some nights I slip between you. The new bride
sleeps buttoned up, slug-smug in polyester. You,
my faithless husband, turn over in your dreams,
and I'm there, ice-cold and seeking out your eyes
and for a moment you brush my lips, and freeze.

GRAVID

The first time was on the Northern Line,
a hot, airless evening, reeking of latex
and aftershave, bodies pressed
in a reluctant multiple confinement.
She got on at Cockfosters, sullen and pale;
I tried not to stare but the swell of her belly –
couldn't tear my eyes from the landscape
of stretched skin straining under the thin
cotton of her dress. One touch,
a quiet cupping of that hard, hot shape;
her scream ripped my ears.
The other passengers tutted, sank back
into their *Evening Standards*.

Much easier, after that; there are places
where they go. The hospital lift,
on the way up to Maternity,
clots of them bulged together
too busy breathing and counting
to notice a grey man clutching dahlias –
a tiny movement as the mechanism jolted,
a muttered apology. In that state
they fill so much space – greedy
with flesh and breath – and the groaning,
the hand in the small of the back, pushing
further towards me – I'd have been a fool
not to take advantage.

These days I'm in control;
there's one I pay. Eight months gone
and tight as a drum – sometimes I think
she'll split. She swaggers in,
with lycra stretched above the hump
her umbilicus like a beige cherry
stuck on for laughs, belly branded by
the track of her linea nigra.
She lets me feel, from breast to pubis,
the jerks and punches under the skin;
she calls it the little bastard. Sometimes
she lets me lick the length of it; I tell her
I think he likes this. He's turning.

ESHNA'S FIRST DAY

Words fail, so we resort to skin –
your hand, bone-cold in mine,
palm on palm. Silently
we examine paints, Lego,
cars. You find my face
and move it, side to side,
your private marble eyes
solemn as jet. I read to you
stories of lions, caterpillars,
trucks. A screen of black
immaculate hair
swings over your face;
you stare at the pictures,
your fingers on my neck.

The other children
bring you puppets, crayons,
blocks. Your lashes flit
for a tremulous second;
you look away.
The bell rings. I unpeel you,
steer you towards the door
watch you look back at me.
Eshna, put your coat on.
You don't reply.
You walk, last in line
into the winter playground
and I watch the slow cold
shadow you.

MARCUS

I found him in a skip, head and torso down, long limbs
pink and hairless. Three hard tugs and he was mine.
He had to be laid flat in the back of the car but,
unlike most men, didn't criticise my driving. I sang
all the way home, bathed him and rubbed him dry,
patted and stroked his fabulous glazed hump.
He never stopped smiling as I chewed his ears
and scraped his belly with my greedy teeth.
He tasted of fresh plastic, with a hint of Badedas.
I gave up Tai Chi, cancelled my counsellor,
rang into work with faked complaints. We embraced,
watched daytime telly with the curtains drawn.
He didn't despise the fat or bald, never bitched
during Richard and Judy, or moaned about my drinking,
my chocolate cravings, my spitting cherry stones.
I loved the way he never sighed or snarled or spoke …
It's been three days. He's even better candle-lit.
I drizzle champagne on his chest as shadows jump.
Here's to us, Marcus. I feast upon his pristine skin,
and fiercely kiss his silent, rigid lips.

WAITING FOR THE FOOT-BINDER

The last evening of toes. She flexes them
so they splay in the dust like stunted fans.
Dusk thickens over the village. Chickens
worry the dirt with their staccato beaks;
she chases them with her younger brother.
He laughs. He is too fast for her.

Tomorrow the foot-binder will sing as she
holds her down, and folds each foot into a fist.

DECK CHAIRS

Split like winter lips, they moulder slowly
like Miss Havisham's feast under a shroud of dust

and what hits is the smell of Ambré Solaire
lingering like a reproach in the canvas. One whiff

and I'm back on a simmering Sussex beach
and you're asleep, slack-jawed, snoring

in time to the sea's slow slap on the shingle.
Here's the ice cream stain that wouldn't shift,

the fossil imprints of buttocks and back,
the sixties slick of early morning Brylcreem.

Driving to the tip this arctic afternoon
I catch my breath, sure I can hear the sea.

POECILIA RETICULATA

All week you trust me with their fragile food,
brittle fragments stinking of old salt.

I pepper the surface of their world
and they thrust upwards, lips flexing,

avoiding my eyes. Sometimes I tap the glass
and they scatter, like balls of mercury.

Sometimes I press my face up close
and mouth silent insults.

They flit disdainfully through arches and castles
as I run my fingers over forbidden surfaces –

mantelpiece, paperweight, books. I study
your desk diary. A clean, assertive script,

an ordered life, with good beech floors
and iridescent fish. My wrist slips.

On the last day, they rise reproachfully
and bob like litter in the cackling water.

THE REAL McCOY

Four floors up, the air is thinner. When I see one
toss her hair, arch her throat, I can scarcely breathe.

Summertime is best, when the heat wraps them up
like luscious parcels. Some are barely dressed.

At night I head for the bar with no mirrors and wait.
I choose a quiet one. Her skin has ripened in the sun

and her neck tastes of vanilla under my tongue.
I fill her full of Bloody Marys and compliments.

We sway home past the Pier, lit up like an x-ray.
There's salt in her hair as my key crunches in the lock.

She wants to know my name. *McCoy*, I tell her.
You're freezing, she complains. *Your fingers are like ice.*

She's drowsy at the end; the spurt of red exhausts her.
I'm cold, she says. I'm too busy drinking to reply.

GRAVITY

Night. I bump over
frost-furred roofs,
then hover at sill level,
peering in on couples
spooned together
under Habitat duvets.

A window-tap
to get them stirring,
to unfurl fingers from breasts
and twitch eyelids,

then off to graze my feet
on black branches
in the wide avenue where
the Doctor lives

and the Swedish girl
asleep in an attic room
dreams of each member
of Boyzone fingering her
in a sauna.

Air slaps between my legs,
cold air stings my teeth.
The town's lit up for me
and thermals buoy me
above the precinct.

But his face, burnt
into my retina; a hand
on my shoulder. Latin
words. Bad handwriting.

I start to lose height.
Telephone wires snare me
over the hospital. I shiver

in their grip, waiting
for light to bruise the sky,
for gravity to ground me.

PICTURE THIS

You come into focus most clearly on windy Mondays,
Grandad's shirt sleeves applauding themselves on the line,
curtains boiling at windows. Your cheeks, normally pale,

slapped red by sudden gusts; I see you bending,
stiff-backed, to retrieve a peg or yank a dandelion,
then your apron snarls itself up and your dress

lifts sharply to reveal the tops of stockings pinching
mottled thighs. I can hold you there for several seconds
until your hair escapes its pins and leaves you blurred.

UNCLE AUBREY

Uncle Aubrey is dying. On the line
pummelled by sheet-steel winds
night-clothes bluster and bulge.

Talk to him, cheer him up says Olwyn
so I tell him I have played on the moor
and seen hawks plucking at mice.

Hands pared to bone, he rubs knuckles
and remembers dead cousins
dead drunk at Christmas.

His head is too heavy for his neck
and his eyes yellow with sickness
too clotted to take me in.

He is dying in Welsh. It is part of me
singing somewhere in my blood
voices of sickness and rain.

FORMICA

Leicester Forest West, between coaches.
In the café, the formica reads *Jason fucked Gemma*.

Sipping bitter tea, I wonder if the striplights
fizzed for a moment when he switched them off,

whether he went on top, whether the sharp arc
of the table sliced her back, whether

iridescent grains of sugar pressed into her flesh,
whether she got up stiffly, shaking out her hair,

stood in the drizzle waiting for the Manchester bus,
while he took out his penknife and began carving.

RESURRECTION

You might crash into the window
like a sudden ragged moth, banging
against the bright glass, or worse,

you'll appear in my mirror, leering
over one shoulder, yellow-skinned,
and bury your fingers in my hair,

or worse still, you'll slouch by my trolley
at the cold meats counter, whisky-foul
and lewd, chewing pastrami. I know

you'll reconstitute head and heart
and lungs and liver and limbs, emerge
from that grey ash, solidify yourself,

breathe into my face. I dream about
the hot grip of your fingers, the dry rasp
of your voice – *listen, it is not finished*.

KEEPSAKES

Each time it's something, slipped inside her bag. At first
she keeps it simple – a marble from the solitaire board,
the innards of his pen, a sock, yellowed with sweat.

One night she hears him singing in the bath, and removes
used plasters from the heels of his trainers. She pats him dry
when he's done, sucks water from the wet snakes of his hair,

and rubs his shoulders. When he takes a lover's call in bed
she slips into his study, removes the polished alabaster egg
that weights girls' numbers to his desk. When she returns

he's sleeping, the white sheets stained and creased
as a bride's gown on a wedding night. Going through his bin
she finds fresh toe-nail clippings and receipts for flowers.

She dresses to the slow beat of his breathing. At home,
she empties out her bag and shapes him on her bed –
flower receipt eyes, sock prick, alabaster heart.

WHAT SHE SEES

She's sent outside while they unpack. Go and see.
First she sees the lizard, its back patterned like carpet,
belly pulsing faster than her breath. She sees it shoot
into a crack, swallowed by dark. Next she sees plums,

blue as day-old bruises, accepting her thumbprint,
their orange flesh slashed open by a heel. Face down
and silent in the scorched grass she watches bees
bristling the lavender to a frenzy. Dry, sullen heat

prickles at her neck and knees; she tracks a beetle
on the path, listens to the splashes and echoes
from a neighbour's pool. She sees her father's face
at a window, the sharp planes of cheek and bone

white from his indoor life. She sees him vanish.
She runs into the sudden cool of dry flagstones
and sees a puddle of clothes by a bed, pale limbs
knotted hard and hot, sudden lights behind her eyes.

KINGFISHER

You split the frozen water with your boot,
disturbed the neat shuttlecock of green and blue
breasting the black. Under the mercury sky

the question quivered between us. Did it freeze
down there, excited by a flicker of fish,
had it pierced the splintered surface, been sucked

into the stiffening stream? You toed it over
and the chestnut-bellied fact of it, the blue
and lucent green of loss smashed home

like the icy shock of drowning. I remembered
when we feathered ourselves up for love.
Today we met in drabber colours, talked clean,

churned fresh mud. It did not change
the freckles on your belly, the piston of your throat,
the way you unpeeled fruit. The sky tore

and peppered us with freezing rain. We sheltered,
sucking our fingertips back to life, ignoring
the flash of iridescence at our feet.

GEOGRAPHY

In the garden of Five, Glynde Close, you let me
peel a map of Africa from your back.
I pulled transparent strips, heard you gasp
as my fingers brushed the new skin underneath.

In those days, I knew where to find you –
squatting low in goal, or hiding under the stairs,
or lounging on your bed drawing armpit hair
on the smiling models in the Empire catalogue.

You showed me the wasps' nest in the shed,
told me they'd smelled my blood and would get me,
let me follow you to the park, then left me
to find my own way home on hot tarmac.

On holiday we squabbled quietly in the back
of the Granada, ignoring the sunflowers
and the huge skies while our parents discussed,
through clenched teeth, the best route south.

When we reached Bandol the sun beat us up
the sea-salt probed cuts and grazes
and we both got lost one day on the beach
eyes bleached by the light on the shingle.

Today you send me a Change of Address;
when I ring you, your voice sounds new,

as if you'd made yourself up. You say, *The garden
is south facing*. There are good schools.

I try to imagine you, positioning your son's goal-posts
on a lawn where the earth will be kicked to dust,
where you'll stand on summer evenings with a glass
of French wine, your shadow impossibly long.

SPIDERS

Fred sees them spinning in the air with silent thread.
He likes their cotton legs, the way they stare him out,
the fragile nets they hang from box to chair. Fred says

look, there's one, but the other children, herding sheep,
cup careful hands round three-legged lambs, fenced in
with chewed green plastic. No-one else hears the crunch

when the fly arrives. Fred draws the latest, green and fat.
Fifteen legs, one head, toes, eyebrows, teeth. The teacher
takes his crayon away and lines him up for lunch.

STORNOWAY HARBOUR

This is the sea of your childhood, diesel-thick,
slapping Styrofoam from the burger bar
against the sides of blue and orange boats.

On the quay, mackerel convulse in buckets,
grinning like madmen; a rictus of scales,
salt-stink. The smell shifts in my stomach.

In the bay, heads gravestone-grey, seals
nose the black water. *They're always there*
you say, and together we watch the men

toss writhing arcs of petrol-blue and slate.
Serene, they duck and surface. They'll wait
forever; Gods, with the patience of stone.

SWEETPEAS

Each evening he braces himself to water sweetpeas
self-seeded and faded as old curtains,
tangled into lacework around the chicken wire fence.

Have some of these, take some he says and presses
frail pastel into my outstretched palms,
the stink of sap leaking from bruised stalks.

We gather them and press our noses into sudden scent
and the heads sag like fretful pensioners,
paper-skinned, waiting for a dry translucent death.

WHITE LIES

I did not take the last of the milk; someone else
spilled red wine over the crossword and
I'm proud to say I've never hit my children.

I wasn't there when the car got scratched.
I never once cheated in a spelling test, never
felt tempted to try a same-sex relationship.

Chopin moves me to tears. I eat green vegetables
for the joy of it. Everything in my shopping bag
I've paid for with my own, hard-earned cash.

A clear conscience is a wonderful comfort.
These are not tears, but drops of glycerine –
a gift from the alien who dead-heads my roses.